Boomps-a-daisy

40 singable songs

A & C Black · London

First published 1986 by A & C Black
(Publishers) Ltd, 35 Bedford Row, London
WC1R 4JH © 1986 A & C Black
(Publishers) Ltd

Piano arrangements by Brian Hunt (20, 24
and 38) and Sue Williams

Cover and illustrations by Tony Blundell

Songs chosen by Peggy Blakeley and Sue
Williams

Music set by Words and Music Graphics,
Southend-on-sea, Essex

Printed in Great Britain by Hollen Street
Press Ltd, Slough, Berkshire

This edition: ISBN 0-7136-5601-8
Also available: Melody edition
ISBN 0-7136-5621-2
Words edition
ISBN 0-7136-5611-5

Contents

1 Lilli Marlene
2 Oh, what a beautiful morning
3 Down at the old Bull and Bush
4 Boomps-a-daisy
5 Spread a little happiness
6 I've got a lovely bunch of coconuts
7 Boiled beef and carrots
8 Wot cher!
9 Maybe it's because I'm a Londoner
10 Keep the home fires burning
11 Lily of Laguna
12 Abdul Abulbul Amir
13 Leaning on a lamp-post
14 The Siegfried Line
15 Georgia on my mind
16 For me and my gal
17 Gone fishin'
18 Get me to the church on time
19 With her head tucked underneath her arm
20 How much is that doggie?
21 Show me the way to go home
22 Kiss me goodnight, Sergeant Major
23 I'm looking over a four leaf clover
24 Bye Bye Blackbird
25 Hey, little hen!
26 On Mother Kelly's doorstep
27 We'll meet again
28 K-K-K-Katy
29 Hernando's Hideaway
30 The blue-tail fly
31 Good-Bye-Ee!
32 When Irish eyes are smiling
33 Oh! Mister Porter
34 Deep in the heart of Texas
35 Oh! Oh! Antonio
36 Waiting at the church
37 The farmyard cabaret
38 Give my regards to Broadway
39 Yankee doodle
40 The Cokey Cokey

1 Lilli Marlene

Hans Leip, Norbert Schultze and Tommie Connor

1 Underneath the lantern by the barrack gate,
Darling, I remember the way you used to wait.
'Twas there that you whispered tenderly,
That you loved me, you'd always be,
My Lilli of the lamplight,
My own Lilli Marlene.

2 Time would come for roll call, time for us
  to part,
Darling, I'd caress you, and press you
  to my heart.
And there 'neath that far off lantern light,
I'd hold you tight, we'd kiss goodnight,
My Lilli of the lamplight,
My own Lilli Marlene.

3 Orders came for sailing somewhere over there,
All confined to barracks was more than I
  could bear.
I knew you were waiting in the street,
I heard your feet, but could not meet,
My Lilli of the lamplight,
My own Lilli Marlene.

4 Resting in a billet just behind the line,
Even tho' we're parted your lips are close
  to mine.
You wait where that lantern softly gleams,
Your sweet face seems to haunt my dreams,
My Lilli of the lamplight,
My own Lilli Marlene.

2 Oh, what a beautiful morning

words: Oscar Hammerstein II
music: Richard Rogers

1 There's a bright golden haze on the meadow,
There's a bright golden haze on the meadow,
The corn is as high as an elephant's eye,
An' it looks like it's climbin' right up to the sky.

    Oh, what a beautiful mornin'
    Oh, what a beautiful day,
    I got a beautiful feelin'
    Ev'rythin's goin' my way.

2 All the cattle are standing like statues,
All the cattle are standing like statues,
They don't turn their heads as they see me ride by,
But a little brown mav'rick is winkin' her eye.
    Oh, what a beautiful mornin'...

3 All the sounds of the earth are like music,
All the sounds of the earth are like music,
The breeze is so busy, it don't miss a tree,
And an' ol' weapin' willer is laughin' at me.
    Oh, what a beautiful mornin'...

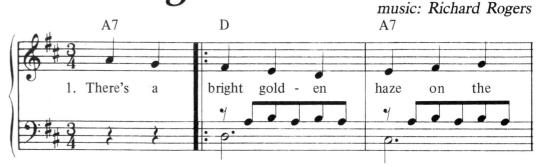

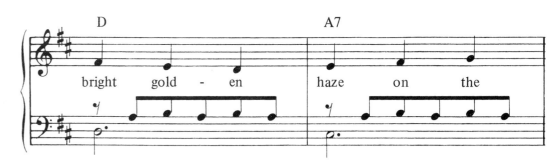

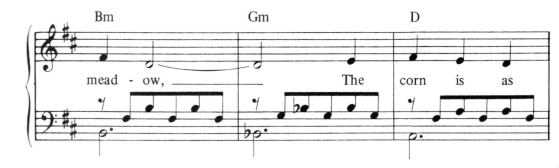

3 Down at the old Bull and Bush

words: Andrew B. Sterling,
Russell Hunting and Percy Krone
music: Harry Von Tilzer

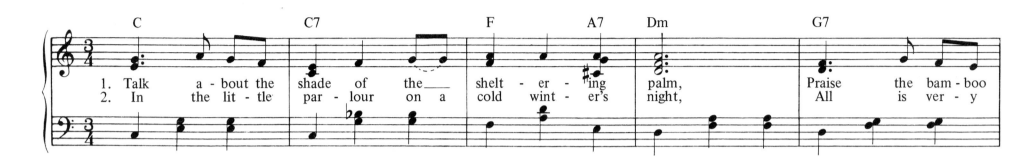

1. Talk a-bout the shade of the___ shelt - er - ing palm, Praise the bam - boo
2. In the lit - tle par - lour on a cold wint - er's night, All is ver - y

tree with it's wide - spread - ing charm. There's a lit - tle nook down our
cheer - ful, so snug and so bright. Nell___ looks at me but now

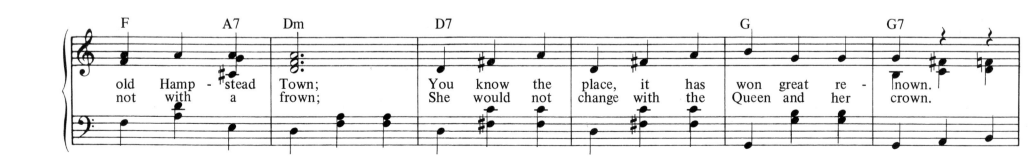

old Hamp - stead Town; You know the place, it has won great re - nown.
not with a frown; She would not change with the Queen and her crown.

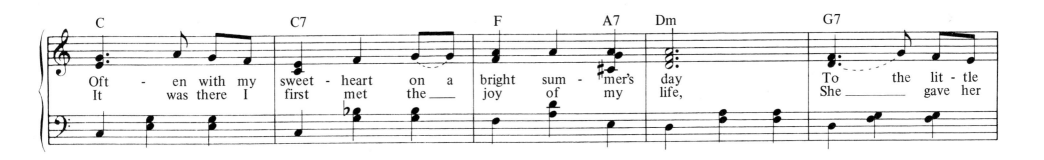

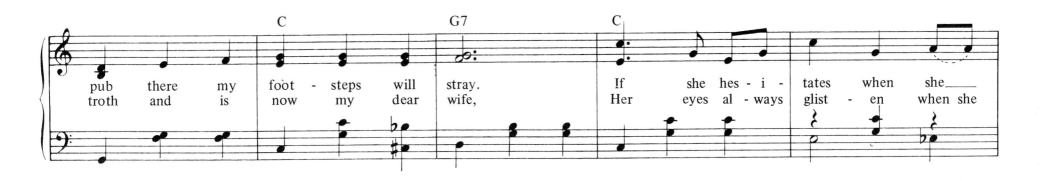

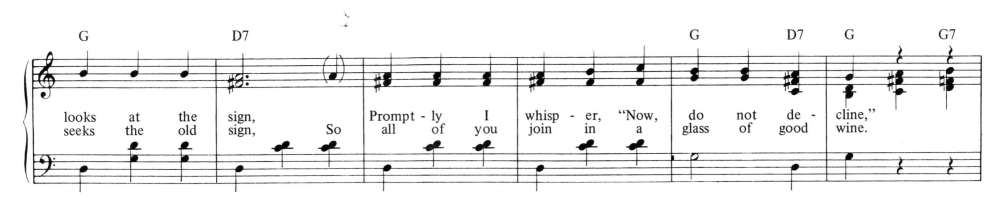

TURN OVER

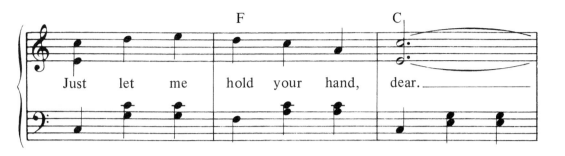

Just let me | hold your hand, | dear. ___

Do, | do

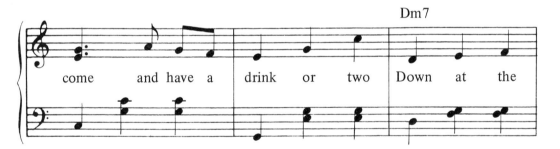

come and have a | drink or two | Down at the

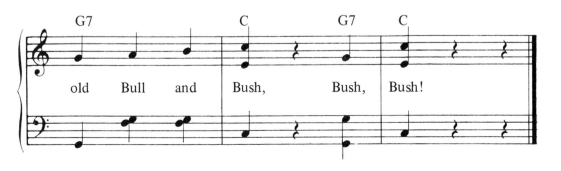

old Bull and | Bush, | Bush, | Bush!

4 Boomps-a-daisy

Annette Mills

1. In the naugh - ty nine - ties la - dies were so gay. In the naugh - ty nine - ties
2. Gent - le - men with whisk - ers whirl the la - dies round, Hop - ing that each bust - le's

this is how they'd play. Waltz - ing as light as a feath - er_____ And
fast-ened safe and sound. Grand - ma says, "Boomp - ing is shock - ing,_____ You

Chorus

bump - ing their bust - les to - geth - er._____ Hands, knees and
might show an inch of your stock - ing."_____

boomps - a - dais - y! I like a bust - le that bends._____

5 Spread a little happiness

words: Clifford Grey
music : Vivian Ellis

TURN OVER

6 I've got a lovely bunch of coconuts

Fred Heatherton

TURN OVER

7 Boiled beef and carrots

Charles Collins and Fred Murray

1 When I was a nipper only six months old,
My mother and my father too,
They didn't know what to wean me on,
They were both in a dreadful stew;
They thought of tripe, they thought of steak,
Or a little bit of old cod's roe,
I said, "Pop round to the old cookshop
I know what'll make me grow.

Boiled beef and carrots,
Boiled beef and carrots.
That's the stuff for your 'Darby-kel',
Makes you fat and it keeps you well,
Don't live like vegetarians
On food they give to parrots,
From morn till night blow out your kite on
Boiled beef and carrots."

2 When I got married to Eliza Brown,
A funny little girl next door,
We went to Brighton for the week,
Then we both toddled home once more.
My pals all met me in the pub,
Said a fellow to me, "Wot cher, Fred.
What did you have for your honeymoon?"
So just for a lark I said,
"Boiled beef and carrots..."

Darby kel: cockney rhyming slang for belly

3 We've got a lodger, he's an artful cove,
  "I feel very queer," he said.
  We sent for the doctor, he came around,
  And he told him to jump in bed.
  The poor chap said, "I do feel bad",
  Then my mother with a tear replied,
  "What would you like for a "Pick-me-up"?"
  He jumped out of bed and cried,
          "Boiled beef and carrots…"

4 I am the father of a lovely pair
  Of kiddies, and they're nice fat boys.
  They're twins, you can't tell which is which,
  Like a pair of saveloys.
  We had them christened in the week.
  When the parson put them on his knee,
  I said, "As they've got ginger hair,
  Now I want their names to be
          Boiled beef and carrots…"

8 Wot cher!

words: Albert Chevalier
music: Charles Ingle

Last week down our alley come a toff,
Nice old geezer with a nasty cough,
Sees my missus, takes his topper off
In a very gentlemanly way.
"Ma'am," says he, "I 'ave some news to tell,
Your rich Uncle Tom of Camberwell,
Popped off recent, which it ain't a sell,
Leaving you 'is little Donkey Shay."

"Wot cher!" all the neighbours cried,
"Who're yer goin' to meet, Bill?
Have you bought the street, Bill?"
Laugh! I thought I should 'ave died,
Knocked 'em in the Old Kent Road!

shay: cart

9 Maybe it's because I'm a Londoner

Herbert Gregg

London isn't everybody's cup of tea,
Often you hear visitors complain.
Noisy, smoky city; but it seems to me
There's a magic in the fog and rain.

Maybe it's because I'm a Londoner
That I love London so.
Maybe it's because I'm a Londoner
That I think of her wherever I go.
I get a funny feeling inside of me
Just walking up and down,
Maybe it's because I'm a Londoner
That I love London Town.

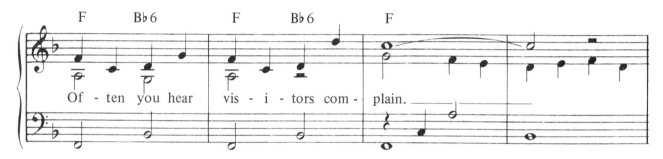

Chorus

May-be it's be-cause I'm a Lon-don-er _____ That I love Lon-don so.

May-be it's be-cause I'm a Lon-don-er _____ That I think of her _____ wher-ev-er I go. I

get a fun-ny feel-ing in - side of me _____ Just walk-ing up and down,

May-be it's be-cause I'm a Lon-don-er That I love Lon-don Town.

10 Keep the home fires burning

words: Lena Guilbert Ford
music: Ivor Novello

Keep the home fires burning,
While your hearts are yearning,
Though your lads are far away
They dream of home.
There's a silver lining
Through the dark clouds shining,
Turn the dark clouds inside out
Till the boys come home.

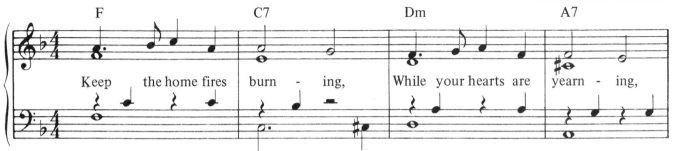

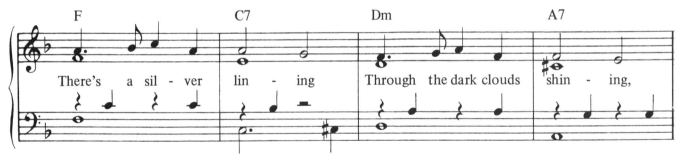

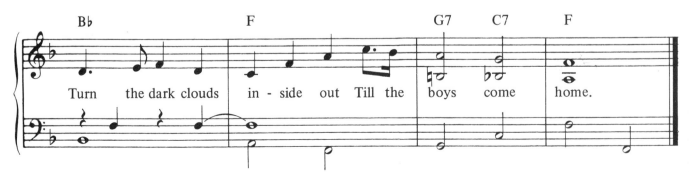

11 Lily of Laguna

Leslie Stuart

*capo on first fret may be used with alternative chords in brackets

12 Abdul Abulbul Amir

1 The sons of the prophet are brave men and bold,
   And quite unaccustomed to fear,
   But the bravest, by far, in the ranks of the Shah
   Was Abdul Abulbul Amir.

2 Now the heroes were plenty and well known to fame
   In the troops that were led by the Tzar,
   And the bravest of these was a man by the name
   Of Ivan Skavinsky Skavar.

3 One day this bold Russian had shouldered his gun,
   And donned his most truculent sneer.
   Down town he did go, where he trod on the toe
   Of Abdul Abulbul Amir.

4 "Young man," quoth Abdul, "Has life grown so dull
   That you wish to end your career?
   Vile infidel, know, you have trod on the toe
   Of Abdul Abulbul Amir."

5 Said Ivan, "My friend, your remarks in the end
   Will avail you but little, I fear,
   For you ne'er will survive to repeat them alive,
   Mr. Abdul Abulbul Amir."

6 "So take your last look at sunshine and brook,
   And send your regrets to the Tzar.
   For by this I imply, you are going to die,
   Count Ivan Skavinsky Skavar."

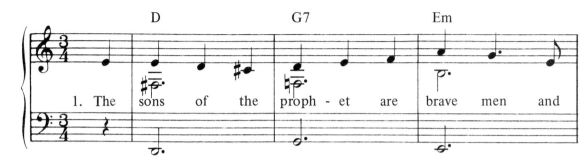

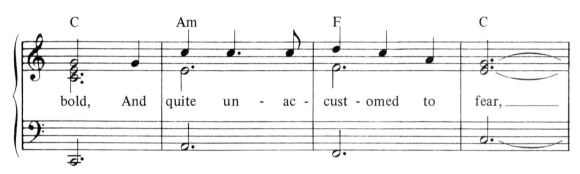

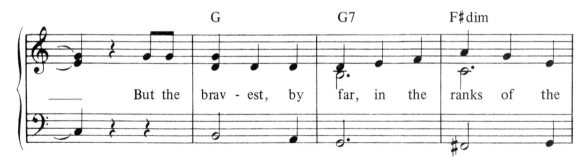

7 They fought all that night 'neath the pale yellow moon;
The din, it was heard from afar.
And huge multitudes came, so great was the fame
Of Abdul and Ivan Skavar.

8 The Sultan drove by in his red-breasted fly,
Expecting the victor to cheeer,
But he only drew nigh to hear the last sigh
Of Abdul Abulbul Amir.

9 Tzar Petrovitch too, in his spectacles blue,
Rode up in his new crested car.
He arrived just in time to exchange a last line
With Ivan Skavinsky Skavar.

10 There's a tomb rises up where the Blue Danube rolls,
And 'graved there in characters clear
Is, "Strangers, when passing, oh pray for the soul
Of Abdul Abulbul Amir."

11 A splash in the Black Sea one dark moonless night
Caused ripples to spread wide and far.
It was made by a sack fitting close to the back
Of Ivan Skavinsky Skavar.

13 Leaning on a lamp-post

Noel Gay

TURN OVER

14 The Siegfried Line

Jimmy Kennedy and Michael Carr

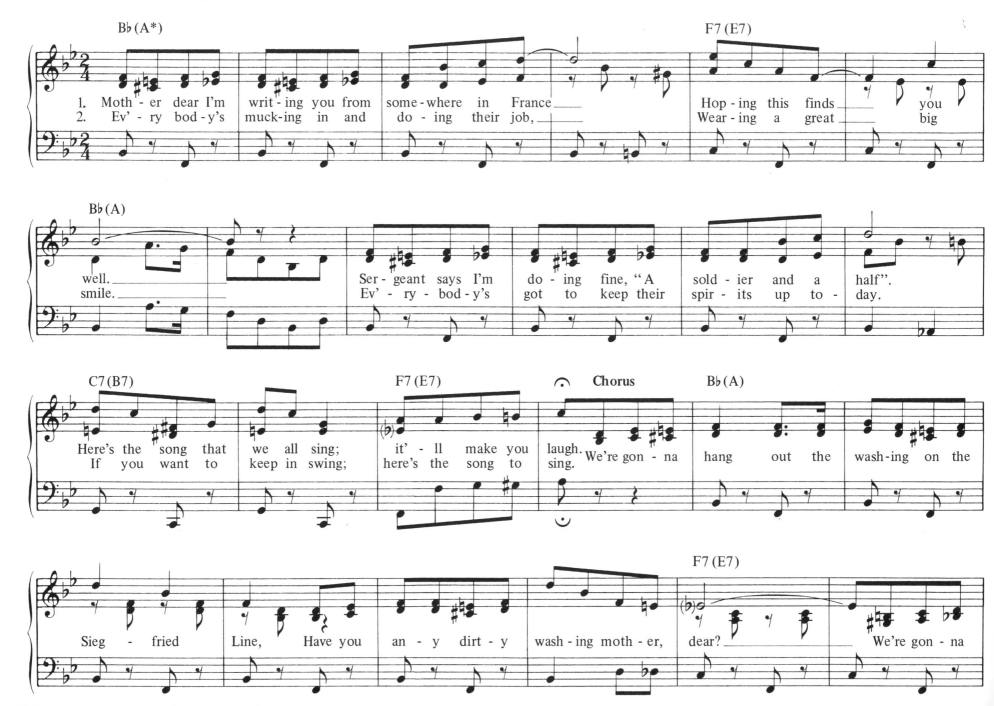

*capo on first fret may be used with alternative chords in brackets

15 Georgia on my mind

words: Stuart Gorrell and Reg Connolly
music: Hoagy Carmichael

16 For me and my gal

words: Edgar Leslie and E. Ray Goetz
music: Geo W. Meyer

1 What a beautiful day for a wedding in May.
See the people all stare at the lovable pair.
She's a vision of joy, he's the luckiest boy.
In his wedding array hear him smilingly say

"The bells are ringing for me and my gal,
The birds are singing for me and my gal.
Everybody's been knowing
To a wedding they're going,
And for weeks they've been sewing,
Ev'ry Susie and Sal.
They're congregating for me and my gal,
The parson's waiting for me and my gal.
And some time I'm goin' to build a little home
For two, for three, for four or more,
In Loveland, for me and my gal."

2 See the relatives there, looking over the pair!
They can tell at a glance it's a loving romance.
It's a wonderful sight, as the fam'lies unite.
Gee! It makes a boy proud as he says to the crowd
"The bells are ringing for me and my gal..."

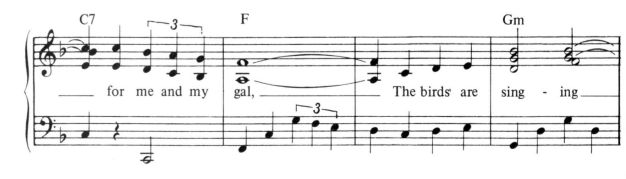

17 Gone fishin'

Nick and Charles Kenny

He's lazy, but he's lovable, we know him like a book.
Any time he can't be found we know just where to look.

Gone fishin', there's a sign above his door.
Gone fishin', he ain't workin' any more.
There's his hoe out in the sun where he left a row half done.
He said, "Hoe-in' ain't no fun." He ain't got no ambition.
Gone fishin', by a shady-wady pool.
I'm wishin' I could be that kind of fool.
I'd say no more work for mine, on my door I'd hang a sign,
Gone fishin', instead of just a-wishin'.

Gone fishin', see him snoozin' by a brook.
Gone fishin', didn't even bait his hook.
There's his hound dog by his side; fleas are bitin' at his hide;
He won't scratch 'em, he's too tired; he ain't got no ambition,
Gone fishin', learnin' fishin' worms to swim.
I'm wishin' he was me and I was him.
Wish I had a 'plane to fly; here's what I'd write in the sky,
Gone fishin', instead of just a-wishin'.

Gone fishin', he don't worry 'bout no wars.
Gone fishin', left his wife to do the chores.
Cows need milkin' in the barn, but he jest don't give a darn.
See his fishin' pole is gone; he's on a secret mission.
Gone fishin' out where peace has never died.
I'm wishin' all the world was by his side,
Then we'd throw our guns away, grab a fishin' pole and say
Gone fishin', instead of just a-wishin'.

18 Get me to the church on time

words: Alan J. Lerner
music: Frederick Loewe

19 With her head tucked underneath her arm

words: Bob Weston and Bert Lee
music: Harris Weston

1. In the Tower of Lon - don, large as life, The ghost of Ann Bo - leyn walks, they de -
2. Some - times gay King Hen - ry gives a spread For all his pals and gals, a ghost - ly
3. Beef - eat - ers all know her well by sight, To see the plight she's in fills her with

- clare. Poor Ann Bo - leyn was once King Hen - ry's wife Un -
- crew. The Heads - man carves the joint and cuts the bread, Then
- grief. And when she wand - ers round their hut at night They

- til he made the Heads - man bob her hair! Ah, yes, he did her wrong long years a -
in comes Ann Bo - leyn to 'queer' the do; She holds her head up with a wild war
al - ways ask her in to share their beef. She thanks them, and then with a puz - zled

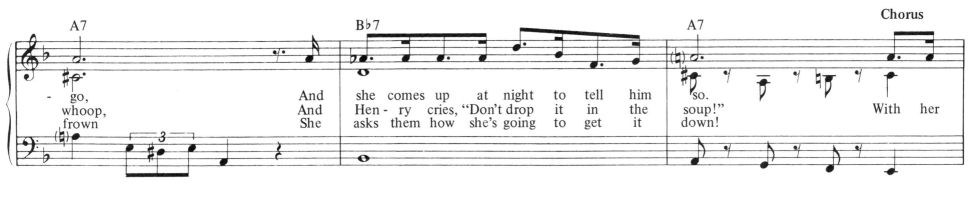

And she comes up at night to tell him so. With her
And Hen - ry cries, "Don't drop it in the soup!"
She asks them how she's going to get it down!

head tucked un - der-neath her arm She walks _____ the Blood - y

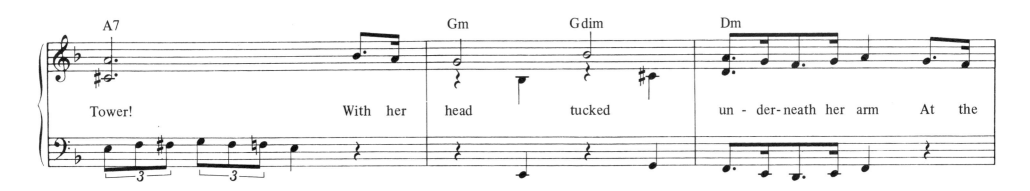

Tower! With her head tucked un - der-neath her arm At the

TURN OVER

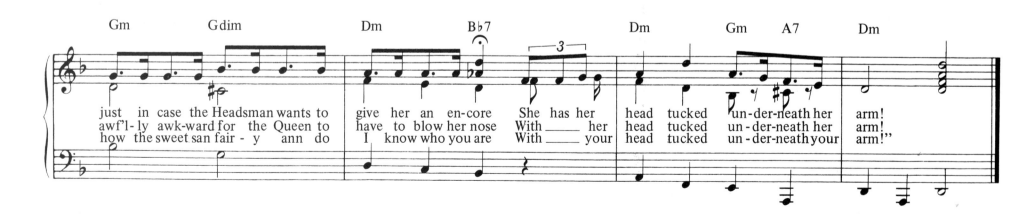

20 How much is that doggie?

Bob Merrill

How much is that doggie in the window?
The one with the waggely tail.
How much is that doggie in the window?
I do hope that doggie's for sale.

I don't want a bunnie or a kitten,
I don't want a parrot that talks,
I don't want a bowl of little fishes;
I can't take a goldfish for walks!

How much is that doggie in the window?
The one with the waggely tail.
How much is that doggie in the window?
I do hope that doggie's for sale.

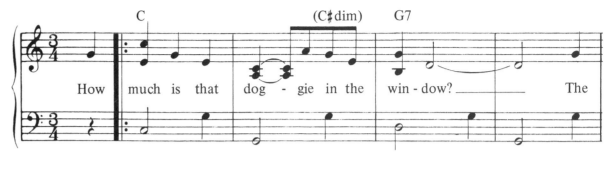

How much is that dog - gie in the win - dow?_____ The

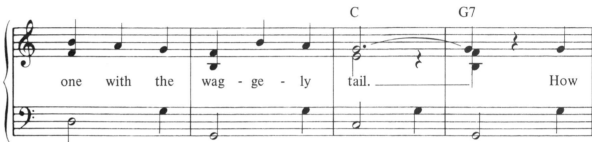

one with the wag - ge - ly tail. _____ How

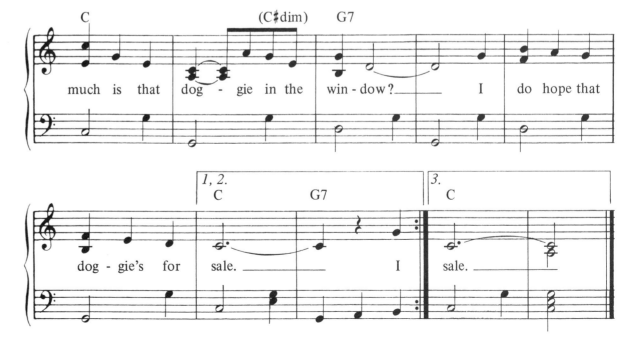

much is that dog - gie in the win - dow?_____ I do hope that

dog - gie's for sale. _____ I | sale. _____

21 Show me the way to go home

Irving King and Hal Swain

When I'm happy, when I'm happy, singing all the while,
I don't need nobody then to show me how to smile.
When've been out on the spree, toddling down the street,
With this little melody everyone I greet;

Show me the way to go home,
I'm tired and I want to go to bed.
I had a little drink about an hour ago
And it's gone right to my head.
Wherever I may roam,
On land, or sea, or foam,
You can always hear me singing this song,
Show me the way to go home.

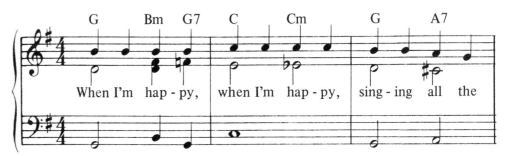

When I'm hap-py, when I'm hap-py, sing-ing all the

while, I don't need no-bod-y then to

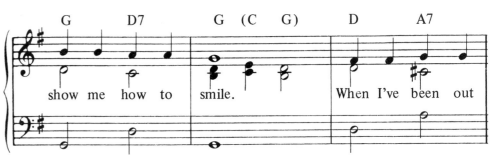

show me how to smile. When I've been out

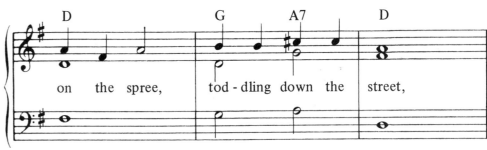

on the spree, tod-dling down the street,

22 Kiss me goodnight, Sergeant Major

Art Noel and Don Pelosi

Pri-vate Jones came in one night, Full of cheer and ve-ry bright, He'd been out all day up-on the spree. He bumped in-to Ser-geant Smeck Put his arms a-round his neck, And in his ear he whis-pered tend-er-ly, "Kiss me good-night, Ser-geant Major, Tuck me in my lit-tle wood-en bed.

23 I'm looking over a four leaf clover

words: Mort Dixon
music: Harry Woods

24 Bye Bye Blackbird

words: Mort Dixon
music: Ray Henderson

Pack up all my cares and woe,

Here I go, singing low.

   Bye, bye Blackbird.

Where somebody waits for me;

Sugar's sweet, so is she.

   Bye, bye Blackbird.

No one here can love and understand me,

Oh what hard luck stories they all hand me.

Make my bed and light the light,

I'll arrive late tonight.

   Blackbird, bye, bye.

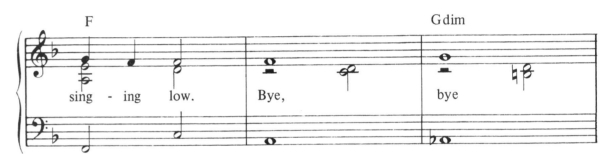

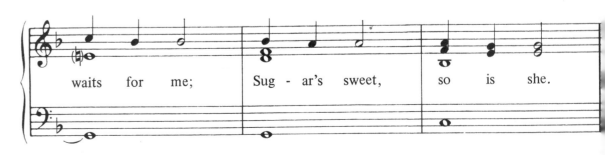

25 Hey, little hen!

Ralph Butler and Noel Gay

1. I had a lot of chick-ens, a large chick-en run, But ow-ing to con-di-tions, I'm
2. I tell her that the butch-er has no meat to-day. I tell her that the fish-es have

now down to one. I give her all the tit-bits, the dear lit-tle thing,
all swim a-way. I tell her I feel hung-ry and weak in the legs,

just to keep her up to scratch I go to her and sing
beg of her sin-cere-ly to get bus-y with the eggs.

Chorus

Hey, lit-tle hen!

When, when, when, will you lay me an egg for my tea?

26 On Mother Kelly's doorstep

Geo A. Stevens

1. I've just been ling - er - ing all a - lone down Par - a - dise Row;___ When
2. The cob - ble stones were a mead - ow sweet to Nel - ly and me.___ The

I was a kid-die I'd a sweet-heart, and down there we would go.___ I'd call her Nel - ly, and she'd
smo - key___ chimney on a house - top was a beau - ti - ful tree.___ And old Brown's don-key was a

call me Joe and we would romp there, hand in hand; Then we'd both sit down on a door - step and we'd___
big baa lamb, and Moth-er Kel - ly in the house. On a wash - day, hold - ing her pail, was Ma - ry the

pict - ure the fut - ure grand. On Moth-er Kel-ly's door - step,___ down Pa - ra-dise Row _____ I'd sit a-long o'
milk-maid___ milk-ing cows. door - step,___ I'm won-der-ing now _____ If li'l ___ gal

27 We'll meet again

Ross Parker and Hugh Charles

1. Let's say good-bye with a smile, dear, Just for a while, dear, we must part. Don't let the part-ing up-set you, I'll not for-get you, sweet-heart.

2. Aft-er the rain comes the rain-bow, You'll see the rain go, nev-er fear. We two can wait for to-mor-row, Good-bye to sor-row, my dear.

Chorus

We'll meet a-gain, don't know where, don't know when, But I know we'll meet a-gain some sun-ny day.

Keep smi-lin' through just like you al-ways do Till the

28 K-K-K-Katy

Geoffrey O'Hara

1 Jimmy was a soldier brave and bold,
Katy was a maid with hair of gold.
Like an act of fate, Kate was standing at the gate
Watching all the boys on dress parade.
Kate smiled, with a twinkle in her eye,
Jim said, "Meet you b-b-bye and bye."
That same night at eight, Jim was at the garden gate,
Stuttering this song to K-K-Kate.

"K-K-K-Katy, beautiful Katy,
You're the only g-g-g-girl that I adore.
When the m-m-m-moon shines,
Over the cow-shed,
I'll be waiting at the k-k-k-kitchen door."

2 No-one ever looked so cute and neat,
No-one could be just as cute and sweet;
That's what Jimmy thought, when the wedding ring he bought;
Dinky little home and all complete.
Jimmy thought he'd like to take a chance,
His heart did a sort of song and dance.
Stepping to a tune, all about the silv'ry moon,
Jimmy followed up his first advance.
    "K-K-K-Katy, beautiful Katy..."

29 Hernando's Hideaway

Richard Alder and Jerry Ross

30 The blue-tail fly

1 When I was young I used to wait
   At master's side and hand his plate,
   And pass the bottle when he got dry,
   And brush away the blue-tail fly.

     Jimmy crack corn and I don't care,
     Jimmy crack corn and I don't care,
     Jimmy crack corn and I don't care,
     Ol' master's gone away.

2 Then after dinner he would sleep,
   A vigil I would have to keep,
   And when he wanted to shut his eye
   He told me, "Watch the blue-tail fly."
     Jimmy crack corn and I don't care

3 One day he rode around the farm,
   The flies so num'rous they did swarm;
   One chanced to bite him on the thigh,
   The devil take the blue-tail fly.
     Jimmy crack corn and I don't care

4 The pony run, he jump and pitch
   And tumble master in the ditch.
   He died, the jury they wondered why;
   The verdict was the blue-tail fly.
     Jimmy crack corn and I don't care

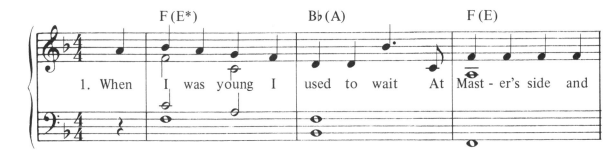

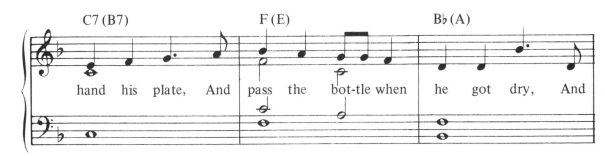

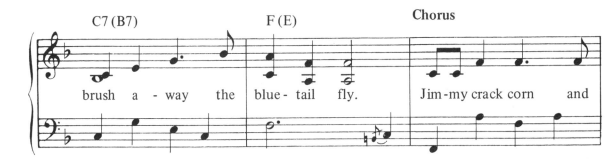

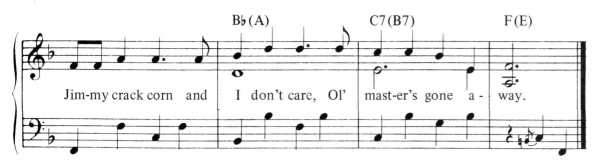

Jim-my crack corn and I don't care, Ol' mast-er's gone a-way.

Bb(A) C7(B7) F(E)

*capo on first fret may be used with alternative chords in brackets

5 They laid him 'neath a 'simmon tree,
   His epitaph is there to see:
   "Beneath this stone I'm forced to lie
   A victim of the blue-tail fly."
      Jimmy crack corn and I don't care

6 Ol' master's gone, now let him rest,
   They say that things are for the best.
   I can't forget till the day I die
   Ol' master and the blue-tail fly.
      Jimmy crack corn and I don't care

'simmon: persimmon, a tree with plum-like fruit

R.I.P
BENEATH THIS STONE
I'M FORCED TO LIE
A VICTIM OF
THE BLUE-TAIL FLY

31 Good-Bye-Ee!

R.P. Weston and Bert Lee

1. Broth-er Bert-ie went a-way to do his bit the oth-er day, With a smile on his lips, and his lieu-ten-ant's pips Up-on his should-er bright and gay. As the train moved out he said, "Re-mem-ber me to all the birds!" Then he wagged his paw, and went a-way to war, Shout-ing out these path-et-ic words, "Good-bye-ee! Good-bye-ee! Wipe the tear, ba-by dear, from your eye-ee. Though it's hard to part, I

know, I'll be tick-led to death to go. Don't cry-ee!___ Don't sigh - ee!___

There's a sil-ver lin-ing in the sky-ee!___ Bon- soir, old thing! Cheer-i - o! Chin, chin! Nah- poo! Tood-le-oo! Good- bye-ee!"___

2 Marmaduke Horatio Flyn, although he'd whiskers round his chin,
In a play took a part, and he touched ev'ry heart
As little Willie in "East Lynne."
As the little dying child,
Upon his snow white bed he lay.
And, amid their tears, the people gave three cheers
When he said, as he passed away,
    "Good-bye-ee! Good-bye-ee!..."

3 At a concert down at Kew some convalescents dressed in blue
Had to hear Lady Lee, who had turned eighty three,
Sing all the old, old songs she knew.
Then she made a speech and said,
"I look upon you boys with pride,
And for what you've done I'm going to kiss each one."
Then they all grabbed their sticks and cried,
    "Good-bye-ee! Good-bye-ee!..."

32 When Irish eyes are smiling

words: Chauncey Olcott and Geo Graff Jnr.
music: Ernest R. Ball

TURN OVER

33 Oh! Mister Porter

words: Thomas Le Brunn
music: George Le Brunn

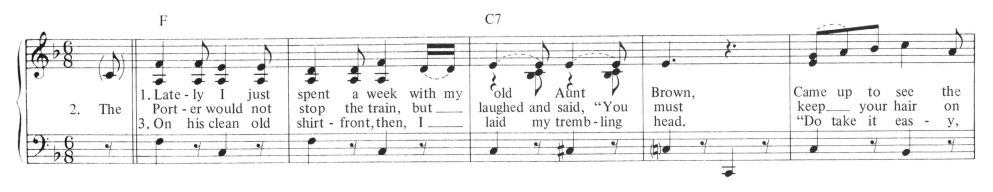

TURN OVER

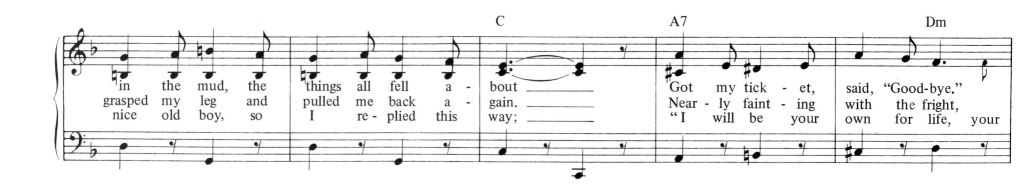

34 Deep in the heart of Texas

words: June Hershey
music: Don Swander

There is a land, a western land,
Mighty wonderful to see.
It is the land I understand
And it's there I long to be.

The stars at night are big and bright,
  Deep in the heart of Texas;
The prairie sky is wide and high,
  Deep in the heart of Texas;
The sage in bloom is like perfume,
  Deep in the heart of Texas;
Reminds me of the one I love,
  Deep in the heart of Texas.

The coyotes wail along the trail,
  Deep in the heart of Texas;
The rabbits rush around the brush,
  Deep in the heart of Texas.
The cowboys cry, "Ki-yip-pee-yi",
  Deep in the heart of Texas;
The doggies bawl, and bawl and bawl,
  Deep in the heart of Texas.

*capo on first fret may be used with alternative chords in brackets

35 Oh! Oh! Antonio

C.W. Murphy and Dan Lipton

1. In quaint na-tive dress an It-al-ian maid, Was deep in dist-ress as the
2. So sad grew the plight of this fair young lass, She'd faint at the sight of an
3. She sought in des-pair for An-to-ni-o, And looked ev'ry-where that she

streets she strayed, Search - ing in ev' - ry part for her false sweet -
ice - cream glass. She'd dream nigh ev' - ry day he'd come back to
thought he'd go. Soon she to pine be - gan as each face she'd

heart And his ice - cream cart. Her Eng - lish was bad it can - not be de -
stay, But he'd fade a - way. Her old hur - dy - gur - dy all day she'd par -
scan For her ice - cream man. She fad - ed a - way, but they say in the

TURN OVER

36 Waiting at the church

words: Fred W. Leigh
music: Henry E. Pether

Introduction

Verse

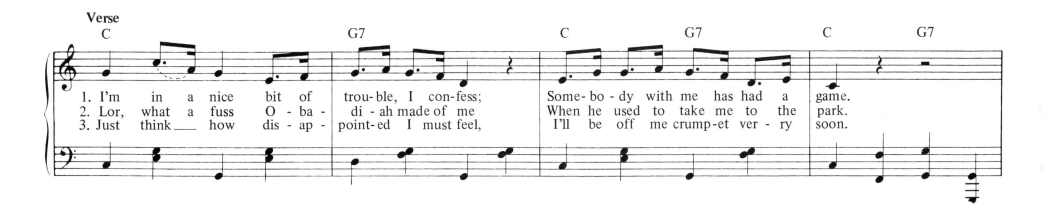

1. I'm in a nice bit of trou-ble, I con-fess; Some-bo-dy with me has had a game.
2. Lor, what a fuss O-ba- di-ah made of me When he used to take me to the park.
3. Just think___ how dis-ap- point-ed I must feel, I'll be off me crump-et ver-ry soon.

I should by now be a proud and hap-py bride, But still I've got to keep my sing-le name.
He used to squeeze me till I was black and blue, When he kissed me he used to leave a mark!
I've lost my hus-band, the one I nev-er had! And I dreamed so a-bout the hon-ey-moon.

TURN OVER

37 The farmyard cabaret

Roy Leslie and Clay Keyes

TURN OVER

38 Give my regards to Broadway

George M. Cohan

TURN OVER

39 Yankee doodle

George M. Cohan

TURN OVER

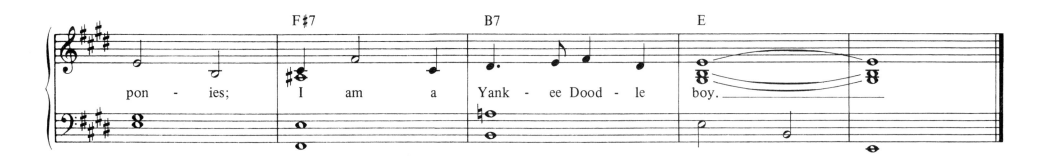

pon - ies; I am a Yank - ee Dood - le boy.

40 The Cokey Cokey

Jimmy Kennedy

*capo on first fret may be used with alternative chords in brackets

The verses continue alternating as many
parts of the body for as long as possible.

Acknowledgements

The following copyright owners have kindly granted their permission for the reprinting of words and music:-

ATV Music Ltd for 4 BOOMPS-A-DAISY

Belwin Mills Music Ltd for 17 GONE FISHIN' and 28 K-K-K-KATY

Box and Cox Publications Ltd for 6 I'VE GOT A LOVELY BUNCH OF COCONUTS

15 GEORGIA ON MY MIND words by Stuart Gorrell, music by Hoagy Carmichael. Copyright© 1930 Southern Music Pub. Co. Inc., U.S.A. Campbell Connelly & Co. Ltd., 78 Newman Street, London W1P 3LA. All rights reserved. Used by permission.
21 SHOW ME THE WAY TO GO HOME by Irving King. Copyright© 1925 Campbell Connelly & Co. Ltd., 78 Newman Street, London W1P 3LA. All rights reserved. Used by permission.
27 WE'LL MEET AGAIN by Ross Parker/Hugh Charles. Copyright© 1939 for all countries by Dash Music Co. Ltd., 78 Newman Street, London W1P 3LA. All rights reserved. Used by permission.
37 THE FARMYARD CABARET by Roy Leslie and Clay Keyes. Copyright© 1932 for all countries by Campbell Connelly & Co. Ltd., 78 Newman Street, London W1P 3LA. All rights reserved. Used by permission.
40 THE COKEY COKEY by Jimmy Kennedy. Copyright© 1942 Kennedy Music Co. Ltd., England. Campbell Connelly & Co. Ltd., 78 Newman Street, London W1P 3LA. All rights reserved. Used by permission.

International Music Publications for 1 LILLI MARLENE, 2 OH WHAT A BEAUTIFUL MORNING, 8 WOT CHER (KNOCKED 'EM IN THE OLD KENT ROAD), 9 MAYBE IT'S BECAUSE I'M A LONDONER, 10 KEEP THE HOME FIRES BURNING, 14 (WE'RE GONNA HANG OUT) THE WASHING ON THE SIEGFRIED LINE, 18 GET ME TO THE CHURCH ON TIME, 19 WITH HER HEAD TUCKED UNDERNEATH HER ARM, 20 THAT DOGGIE IN THE WINDOW, 22 KISS ME GOODNIGHT, SERGEANT MAJOR, 26 ON MOTHER KELLY'S DOORSTEP, 29 HERNANDO'S HIDEAWAY, 31 GOODBYE-EE, 33 OH MISTER PORTER, 35 OH OH ANTONIO, 38 GIVE MY REGARDS TO BROADWAY and 39 YANKEE DOODLE BOY

International Music Publications and Redwood Music Ltd for 3 DOWN AT THE OLD BULL AND BUSH, 5 SPREAD A LITTLE HAPPINESS, 16 FOR ME AND MY GAL, 23 I'M LOOKING OVER A FOUR LEAF CLOVER, 24 BYE BYE BLACKBIRD and 32 WHEN IRISH EYES ARE SMILING

Noel Gay Music Company Ltd for 13 LEANING ON A LAMP-POST and 25 HEY LITTLE HEN

Southern Music Publishing Company Ltd for 34 DEEP IN THE HEART OF TEXAS

Every effort has been made to trace and acknowledge copyright owners. If any right has been omitted, the publishers offer their apologies and will rectify this in subsequent editions following notification.

Guitar Chords

x   string should not be sounded
o   open string
    "barre" – two or more strings held down by one finger

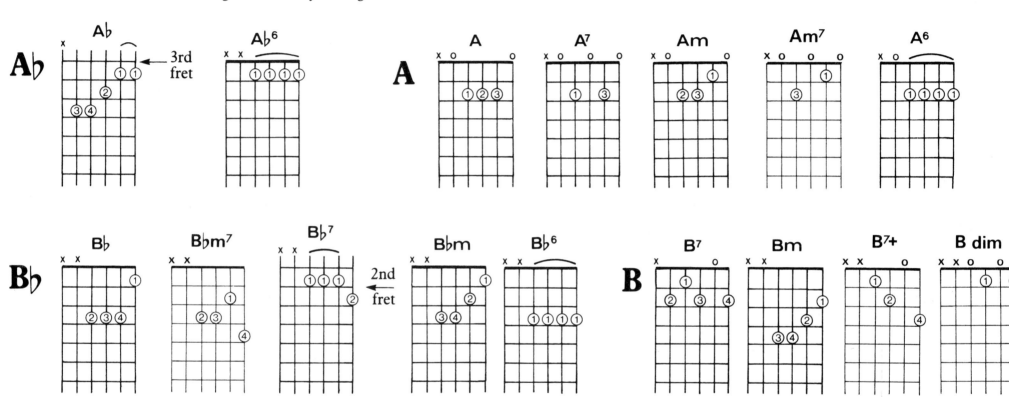

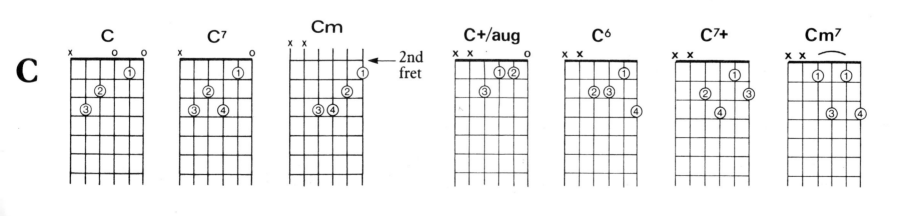

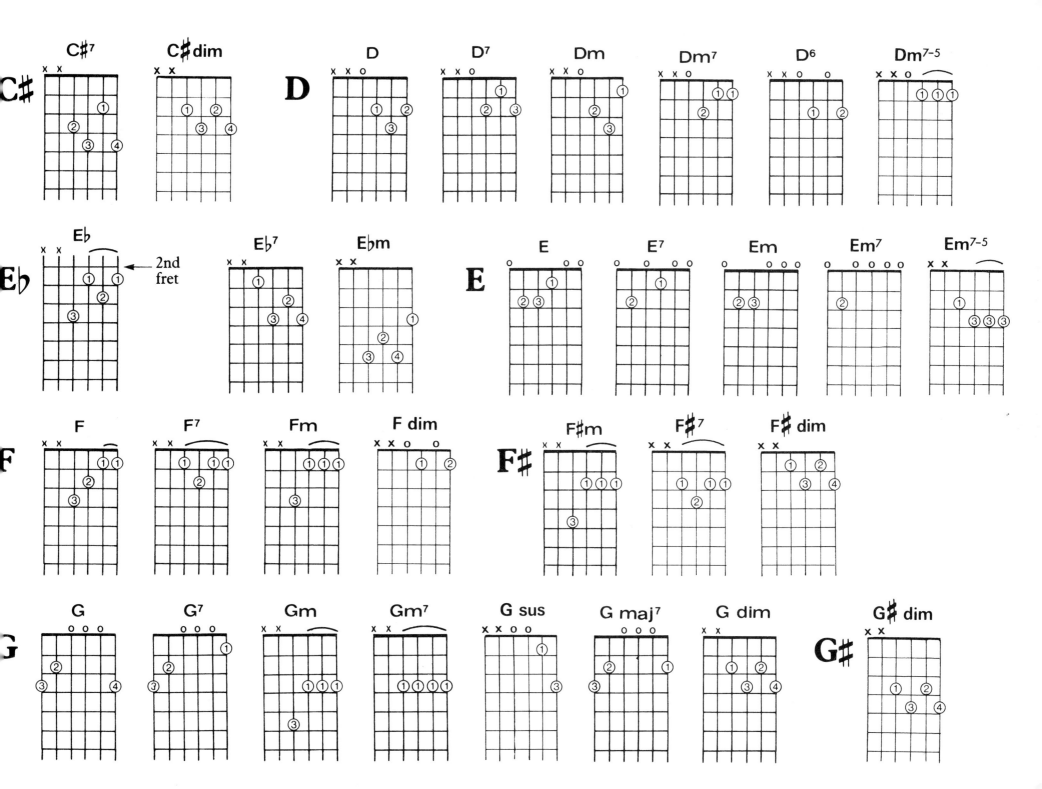

Index of first lines

Animals down on the farm, The, 37
Brother Bertie went away, 31
Did you ever see two Yankees, 38
Down at Barney's Fair, 6
Farewell ev'ry old familiar face, 23
He's lazy, but he's lovable, 17
How much is that doggie? 20
I had a lot of chickens, 25
I know a dark secluded place, 29
I'm getting married in the morning, 18
I'm in a nice bit of trouble I confess, 36
I'm the kid that's all the candy, 39
In quaint native dress an Italian maid, 35
In the naughty nineties, 4
In the Tower of London large as life, 19
I've just been lingering all alone, 26
Jimmy was a soldier brave and bold, 28
Keep the home fires burning, 10
Last week down our alley come a toff, 8
Lately I just spent a week with my old Aunt Brown, 33
Leaning on a lamp, maybe you think I look a tramp, 13
Let's say goodbye with a smile dear, 27
London isn't everybody's cup of tea, 9
Melodies bring memories that linger in my heart, 15
Mother dear I'm writing you from somewhere in France, 14
Pack up all my cares and woe, 24
Private Jones came in one night, 22
She's my lady love, 11
Sons of convention are brave men and bold, The, 12
Talk about the shade of the sheltering palm, 3
There is a land, a western land, 34
There's a bright golden haze on the meadow, 2
There's a tear in your eye, 32

Underneath the lantern by the barrack gate, 1
What a beautiful day for a wedding in May, 16
When I'm happy, when I'm happy, singing all the while, 21
When I was a nipper only six months old, 7
When I was young I used to wait, 30
You put your left arm out, 40